LET THE GAMES BEGIN

A Guide To Self-Exploration and Team Building Activities

RUTH FRISZ PH.D
JOE BERTOLINO ED.D
UGO EZE

iUniverse, Inc.
Bloomington

Let The Games Begin
A Guide to Self-Exploration and Team Building Activities

Copyright © 2012 by Ruth Frisz, Ph.D, Joe Bertolino, Ed.D, and Ugo Eze.

All rights reserved. No part of this book may be used or reproduced by any means, graphic, electronic, or mechanical, including photocopying, recording, taping or by any information storage retrieval system without the written permission of the publisher except in the case of brief quotations embodied in critical articles and reviews.

iUniverse books may be ordered through booksellers or by contacting:

iUniverse
1663 Liberty Drive
Bloomington, IN 47403
www.iuniverse.com
1-800-Authors (1-800-288-4677)

Because of the dynamic nature of the Internet, any web addresses or links contained in this book may have changed since publication and may no longer be valid. The views expressed in this work are solely those of the author and do not necessarily reflect the views of the publisher, and the publisher hereby disclaims any responsibility for them.

Any people depicted in stock imagery provided by Thinkstock are models, and such images are being used for illustrative purposes only.
Certain stock imagery © Thinkstock.

ISBN: 978-1-4759-3519-6 (sc)
ISBN: 978-1-4759-3520-2 (ebk)

Library of Congress Control Number: 2012912074

Printed in the United States of America

iUniverse rev. date: 07/11/2012

TABLE OF CONTENTS

Introduction ix

Opening Activities 1

"Facts That Click" 1
"If You Were" 2
"Name Game" 3
"Public Announcement" 4
"Representations" 4
"Rollin' on a Fortune" 5
"Sentences and Stories" 6
"Slices of Life" 7
"That Thing About You" 7
"The Unexplored" 8
"This Is Who We Are" 8
"Time Periods" 9
"What's Your Sign?" 9
"When You Wish Upon a Star" 10

Self Exploration Activities 13

"A Face in the Crowd" 13
"All Alone" 15
"Alternate Ending" 16
"Book of Life" 17
"Card of Memories" 18

"Changes Within" 20
"Coat of Arms" 21
"Cycles of Life" 22
"The Genie & Me" 23
"Great Escape" 24
"Guess Who" 25
"Guided Imagery" 26
"Headband Exercise" 27
"Hot Seat" 29
"I Want to. I Wouldn't Dare." 30
"If I Had a Million Dollars" 32
"Inside Out" 33
"Jekyll & Hyde" 34
"Last Chance" 35
"Life's Successes" 37
"Mirror and Me" 37
"My New Neighbor" 39
"Past Experience" 40
"Personal Ads" 41
"Personal Pyramid" 42
"Pictures and Goals" 43
"Pieces of Me" 44
"Rituals" 45
"Rolling on a Fear" 46
"Spin the Bottle" 47
"Taking Sides" 49
"Things We've Lost" 50
"Wall Around Our Heart" 51
"War" 53
"Wheel of Reflections" 54
"Where Do I Belong?" 55

Team Building 57

"Balloon Toss" 58
"Building a Utopia" 59

"Changing the Game" 60
"Dream World" 62
"Egg Drop" 63
"Group Introduction" 64
"Marshmallow Tower w/ Roles" 65
"Our Time Together" 67
"Skits" 68
"Stranded With Strangers" 69
"Survival Scramble" 70
"Whatever Floats Your Boat" 71

Relaxation Activities 75

"Bed Time Story" 76
"Embarrassing Revelations" 76
"Musical Chairs" 77
"Speedy Squirrel" 78
"Twilight Zone" 79
"Words From the Wise" 80

Closing Activities 83

"Discovery" 84
"Graveyard" 84
"Hard Letting Go" 86
"Into Reality" 87
"Life Saver" 87
"Medal of Honor" 88
"Our Avatars" 88

Conclusion 91

INTRODUCTION

"Whatever you are, be a good one."—Abraham Lincoln

Quick Tips from the Authors

Dr. Ruth says:

The activities found in this manual were developed over thirty years in the context of a service learning educational experience, which was part of the Peer Program at Queens College. The Program consists of three credit-bearing courses: "Introduction to Counseling and Advisement", "Practicum in Counseling and Advisement", and "Advanced Practicum in Counseling and Advising" The first course is an educational training course where the students who are selected to become Peer Counselors are trained in counseling techniques and skills as well as communication and interviewing techniques. During the second semester course, the students actually do peer counseling and this is one of their practicum experiences. The emphasis in this course is supervision by licensed staff psychologists and counselors, and topic-related discussions on such issues as stress, depression, suicide, culture, and adolescence to name a few. The third and final semester of the program involves continued development of counseling skills, learning how to supervise and teach, the center piece of this course is the semi-annual retreat which is a requirement for all the students in the program.

Ruth Frisz, Ph.D, Joe Bertolino, Ed.D, and Ugo Eze

The third semester students create, plan, organize, implement and evaluate the weekend under the supervision of the professor who teaches the course and is also the program coordinator. The Director of Counseling assists with this project and also trains the small group facilitators. The weekend is the term project for the third semester students. Approximately 60 students and 4 staff attend this weekend every semester.

The weekends focus on leadership development, interpersonal communication and team building. The Peer Counselors, throughout the years, have participated in a series of activities designed around a specific theme. These are conducted in large and small groups and each are processed by group facilitators who are students and are trained in group facilitation prior to the weekend.

The weekends allow the participants to come together for an opportunity to learn about and participate in an educational activity that encourages collaboration and involvement between and among the students, the faculty coordinator and the professional counselors.

This model and these activities can be used by many different types of organizations including, but not limited to educational institutions, businesses, non-profit organizations, and religious institutions.

The activities lend themselves to adjustments and revisions depending on the goals of the workshop, conference, weekends or in-service meetings. This manual is designed to offer ideas and suggestions to those who want to provide this kind of opportunity to their employees, students, administrators, management teams or others.

Dr. Joe says:

If there is any advice I can give a program organizer, facilitator or participant when approaching any of these activities is to HAVE

FUN! Assembling a program and participating in it shouldn't feel like a chore. Regard it as an opportunity. In a fast paced society where our technology is only hurtling us faster into a realm of impersonal cyber communication, sitting down with several other people and expressing thoughts and emotions, revealing aspirations and fears, and coming to terms with victories and losses, are a rarity. So cherish this opportunity.

Ugo says:

During my tenure at Queens College, I was presented with the opportunity to become involved in various programs that facilitated leadership training and self-exploration. My long-term participation with these programs has equipped me with direct knowledge of the student/participant point of view. While assembling this book, I was able to operate from a facilitator point of view. I am now able to speak candidly from both standpoints. Through this, I have come across a few simple ideas that will aid in the creation of a successful program. Now let's get this party started!

Kicking Things Off

So you intend on creating a program for a conference, seminar, meeting, gathering, shindig or whatever you prefer to call it? This is great! However, some may now wonder, "where do I go from here?" but have no fear! We are here to assist you in this endeavor. We have listed a few concepts to consider when formulating your program. If something appeals to you and fits your needs, use it. If it doesn't, leave it and move on. Agreed? Awesome. Let's get this party started.

Setting a Goal

This is a concept that is often overlooked by many directors when creating a program, conference, seminar etc. Simply having a goal in mind will leave no room for ambiguity when it's time to determine if your goal was reached. It is better to work all that out from the beginning. State your goal for the program and then work directly towards it through the exercises with assistance by the facilitators and the participants. Precision can produce wonders. For instance, if the goal is to facilitate leadership skills or team building, then the activities chosen should reflect this.

Creating a Theme

Creating themes will aid in establishing and reaching the goals established. There are two different types of themes which are "subject" and "concept" themes.

The **subject theme** concerns the type of topics that will be addressed during the program. Possible subject theme choices can be about personal values, culture (however you choose to define it), religion, understanding social biases, stereotypes, communication, decision making, or even learning to relax.

It is imperative that you identify what type of culture you are aiming to reach. For example, if you are the CEO of a financial advising company, who is looking to boost employee morale, it may not be very productive to discuss underground street fighting culture and etiquette. While it may be very entertaining and enlightening, it is a better idea to discuss concepts related to your field.

Selecting a **concept theme** is a great way to have fun with programming. Some of the themes from our past retreats were Time Travel, Survivor, Hollywood Films, Island Vacations, Time

Capsules, Around the World in 3 Days, The Mask, Shakespeare, and Fairy Tales to name a few.

For example, if a program director wants to explore self reliance and team work, they may choose a concept such as "Survivor". One version to play out the Survivor concept is to relate it to the very successful television show. On the show, contestants are stranded on a "deserted" island and are forced to work with each other in an effort to survive. The objective is to become the sole survivor and win a huge cash prize. For the program, we opted to *not* offer prizes for backstabbing and conspiring. We focused on the issues of self reliance and codependency that would arise through being stranded on an island with others and working on a solution as a team.

During a program with such a concept theme, values and judgments are also explored. Will the group adopt a *democratic mentality* or will it turn into *survival of the fittest* on the island? The opportunity for exploration is endless when you put a group into a situation and allow them to act.

Time Frames and Group Numbers

For all of our exercises, we have suggested time frames and the number of participants that were involved, per group. The average number of participants in the entire group was roughly 60. The participants were often separated into groups of 6-8 and this worked very well. When a small group number begins to exceed 8 participants, it becomes tougher to maintain a deeper level of intimacy and effective communication. It also jeopardizes the chance of everyone's voice being heard and understood. When conducting activities where personal information is being shared, it is important to keep the group numbers from becoming too large in order to insure privacy and provide intimacy.

However the time allocation and number of groups/group members for each activity all depends on the number of participants and facilitators present. It is up to the program director or facilitators to designate the appropriate time limits that will work best for their programs. The same rule applies for the numbers of people placed within the small groups.

Joining the Gang

While it is important for the facilitators to remain distinguished as "facilitators", it is extremely beneficial for the facilitators to participate in the activities when appropriate. It is the same concept of the politician going around and shaking the hands of people in his/her constituency. The facilitator will become a more involved and trusted figure which will lead to the participants responding more candidly to the events of the program. As facilitators, it is tempting to become the voice of authority and just bark out directions. However, world history illustrates how people tend to want to overthrow dictators. Believe us, that is not what you want. A facilitator should aim to be a role model by participating in the small groups. The facilitator will be able to demonstrate what is expected of the participants. This will also build a level of trust and comfort in the group and will hopefully facilitate openness and honesty among the group members.

Freedom Within the Structure

When it comes to creating a program centered on leadership, communication, self exploration, intra and inter group understanding and team building, no two programs are alike. While the activities and time frames may remain the same, the participants and the experiences they bring with them will always produce something new. Perhaps it will be something surprising but don't be alarmed! This is a good thing. A program that facilitates monotony is a program waiting to be trashed and burned. Be open and ready for the twists and turns that may present themselves as the activities and program goes on. It is ever so important to "live in the moment" while being conscious of the structures in place.

The directors and facilitators are the connection between the planned itinerary and the actual events that happen during the program. They must remain cognizant of the necessity and importance of incorporating both aspects within a program.

Be Open and Have Fun

The activities that are presented in this book are not set in stone. If an activity calls for there to be 5 red straws in the middle of a circle, and you don't want to use straws or can't find any, this is fine! If you want to say forget the straws in total and prefer a square over a circle, go with that! There is never one correct way to do things especially when it comes to activities such as these. The way we have an activity setup in this book may not work well for the group and/or location you are working with. Take the liberty to alter it to fit your needs or come up with an entirely new activity if need be. If the activity works, is enjoyable and helps reach the desired goal for the group, then it is worth using.

"Character is so largely affected by association that we cannot afford to be indifferent as to who or what our friends are."—Unknown

OPENING ACTIVITIES

"If you only do what you know you can do, you never do very much"—Tom Krause

The purpose of any ***opening activity*** is to get people talking and sharing, getting to know each other and establish a comfort level to begin the "meat" of the experience and accomplish the goals. If this is accomplished, the activity has done its job. Even if they're talking about how much they hated the activity and how terrible the facilitators are, they're still talking and sharing! That's always a good thing! Silence is the only indication of a poor result or hesitant participants but that is easily rectified as the sharing continues.

"Facts That Click"

Goal: to allow the group to share personal facts about themselves.

Materials: Lego pieces and a bag.

Directions: (45 minutes to an hour)

Fill a bag with Lego pieces of various colors. Each Lego color corresponds to a different category. For example:

Red= culture
Blue= family

Yellow= leisure/hobbies
Gray=relationships
White= career/goals

Everyone will pick a Lego block. Each person will introduce themselves, and then state a fact about them pertaining to the color/category of the Lego piece they've picked up. They will then place the Lego piece on the base and return to their seat. The facilitator will then call another person to do the same and so on.

Large Group Facilitation Questions:

How did it feel to present in front of the entire group?
What categories were harder to reveal things about yourself than others?

"If You Were"

Goal: To allow the participants to share random facts about themselves.

Directions: (45 minutes to an hour)

The nature of this activity is simple. The facilitator asks every participant a question. The facilitator can have a set of base questions or can have as many questions as there are participants. (it is okay to repeat questions) All participants should be told to stand. When a person is called to answer a question, they should step forward and sit down after they have answered their question.

Here are a few sample questions . . .

If you were a movie what would the title be?
If you were portrayed in a movie, what actor/actress would play you?
If you were an animal which animal would you be?

If you were a smell, what would you smell like?
If you were a town, village, or city, which one would you be?
If you were to meet a historical figure, who would it be?
If you were a TV show, which would it be?
If you were a car, which one would you be?
If you were a song, which one would you be?
If you were a clothing article, which one would you be?

Large Group Facilitation Question:

How easy or difficult was it to answer your questions in front of the large group?

"Name Game"

Goal: Icebreaking.

Directions: (45 minutes to an hour)

Sit the entire group in a circle or semi circle. Everyone should be able to see each person participating. The first person will say their name, preceded by a word that describes them. For instance, "Unstoppable Ugo", "Jazzy Joseph" or "Ravishing Ruth" would all be valid submissions.

After the first person goes, the second person will recite the first person's word and name, and declare theirs. The third person will do the same and so on and so on.

This is how it will look on paper . . .

Ugo: Hey guys. I'm **Unstoppable Ugo.**

Joseph: Unstoppable Ugo, I'm **Jazzy Joseph.**

Ruth: Unstoppable Ugo, Jazzy Joseph and I'm **Ravishing Ruth**

Large Group Facilitation Question:

How did it feel to have to remember everyone's name and adjectives?

"Public Announcement"

Goal: Participants are given the opportunity to divulge information about them that will allow the other group members to understand their personality better.

Directions: (45 minutes)

The facilitators and participants will all introduce themselves and state something about themselves that is integral to understanding their character and personalities.

Example: Hi guys. My name is Andrew and I have a very sarcastic personality.

Large Group Facilitation Questions:

How did you feel about this exercise?
What made you choose this one thing?
How did you feel about sharing this in front of the group?
What have you learned from other's responses?

"Representations"

Goal: Participants will have the opportunity to introduce themselves and share aspects of themselves with the group through picture representations.

Materials: Drawing paper and drawing utensils.

Directions: (45 minutes to an hour)

The facilitator will instruct the group to draw a picture of something that can represent them. After they have completed this task, the participants will go around and introduce themselves and explain how the picture represents them.

Large Group Facilitation Questions:

How did you feel about choosing what to draw? What were your reactions to what someone else drew?
What other picture would you like to draw? What is it?
What else would anyone like to add?

"Rollin' on a Fortune"

Goal: The activity is designed to allow the participants to share what their future goals and aspirations are.

Material: Several pieces of paper rolled up like a scroll.

Directions: (45 minutes to an hour)

The facilitator will announce to the group that they have done their research on the lives and habits of all the participants and have future predictions of their lives written down on rolled up sheets of paper. We will call it a "fortune roll". These fortune rolls should be placed in a basket where everyone will be able to see them.

The fortune rolls should be blank except for the name of the participant written on the outside of the roll. The facilitator should begin to go around and ask everyone questions such as . . .

Knowing yourself and your habits, what do you think your "fortune roll" says about your future goals?
What have you done to pursue this goal?
How badly do you want to achieve this goal?

DO NOT give the rolls to the participants until the ending of the program you are facilitating. Once the fortune rolls have been distributed, have the participants open them up. After they see that there is nothing written inside of it, proceed to hand out writing utensils. Inform them that they are the only people who can construct their own fortune and they should do so now. Have them keep the rolls as a reminder of the power they have over their lives.

"Sentences and Stories"

Goal: To allow the participants to work together in creating and telling a story.

Directions: (1 hour)

One person will begin the story with a sentence of his or her own choice. The next person will add one sentence to the story. Continue around the room until everyone has had a chance to speak. The last person will end the story.

(The facilitator can select a topic or direction for the story to go.)

Large Group Facilitation Questions:

How did you feel about the exercise?
What did you like about the exercise?
What didn't you like about the exercise?
What did you think of the story?

"Slices of Life"

Goal: To allow participants to introduce themselves by sharing what their major focus in life is, at the moment.

Materials: A circle of cardboard cut up into several pieces and markers. There must be one piece for every participant.

Directions: (45 minutes to an hour)

The facilitator will hand out the cardboard slices to the participants and instruct them to write down what their main focus in life is right now. Answers can range from *making money, raising my kids, finding a girlfriend, religion, losing weight, or buying a pair of $800 sunglasses*. After the person has shared what is on their slice, they will place it in the middle of the room to form a full circle.

Large Group Facilitation Questions:

What do you think about this being your main focus? How come?
What do you think about what is in the pie in total?
How do you feel about your focus, when viewing everyone else's? How come?

"That Thing About You"

Goal: To allow participants to share qualities about themselves with the group that they believe to be important in their lives.

Directions: (45 minutes to an hour)

The facilitator should keep the large group together and have everyone answer the given questions.

Questions for participants:

What characteristic about yourself do you feel is most memorable about you? How come?
How does this trait affect your interaction with others? (Optional)
What other trait would you choose to stand out about you? How come? (Optional)
What else would anyone would like to say?

"The Unexplored"

Goal: This opening activity allows for the participants to introduce themselves while sharing unexplored ambitions and goals.

Directions: (45 minutes to an hour)

The facilitator will initiate the activity by asking the entire group "If you had the freedom to explore something you've never done before, what would it be?" It can be an activity, relationship, religion, culture, career, etc.

Large Group Facilitation Questions:

How difficult was it to think about uncharted territory that you hadn't yet experienced?
What are the obstacles in life that prevent you from having the "unlimited freedoms" to explore your goals?
How did other people's responses relate to your own aspirations?

"This Is Who We Are"

Goal: This icebreaker allows for participants to share information about themselves through items they have brought with them.

Directions: (45 minutes)

Ask the entire large group about "something they've brought with them that is distinctly them and what makes it so."

Large Group Facilitation Questions:

How did it feel introducing yourself through something you brought with you?
What kind of connection do you think you will feel when you see someone with their object later on?
What else would you like to share?

"Time Periods"

Goal: This is a simple opening activity that allows the participants to learn more about each other.

Direction: (45 minutes)

In this exercise, the facilitator will instruct the participants to go around and introduce themselves to the group. Along with their introduction, the participants are to answer the question "If you could live in any time period, which one would it be and how come?"

Allow time for questions at the end of the activity but questions are not essential to the exercise.

"What's Your Sign?"

Goal: Participants will be able to look at their lives and determine what road sign best represents where they are in their lives.

Materials: Drawing paper and drawing utensils

Directions: (45 minutes to an hour)

The facilitator will hand out a pen and paper, if needed, to all the participants. They should be asked to draw what road sign best represents the stage they are in their life. The signs can vary from "dead end" to "children at play" or "last exit before toll".

Once everyone is done drawing their signs, the facilitator will select someone to begin with. The "chosen one" will explain their sign and how it pertains to their life, and then the next person will go and so on.

Large Group Facilitation Questions:

How did you feel about this exercise?
How did you feel about sharing this representation of you?
If you could pick a second sign, which would it be? How come?

"When You Wish Upon a Star"

Goal: The purpose of this activity is to allow the participants the opportunity to introduce themselves to each other as well as learning something about the other participants.

Materials: Paper cut outs of stars with names of participants on the stars. If you have 10 participants, then have 10 stars, 100 participants, 100 stars, 1,000 participants.

Directions: (1 hour and 15 minutes)

Each Person will have a star with their name on it. One person will be called on to begin the exercise. They are to take the star with their name and complete the following sentence . . .

"When I wish upon a star, I wish for _____ because _____."

Once that sentence is completed, the person then picks another star and reads out the name of the next person who will undergo the same process. The individual task should be completed in less than 60 seconds. It's an icebreaker, not a therapy session.

Large Group Facilitation Questions:

How did it feel to be asked about your wishes?
How might your wish change 5 years from now?
What does your wish tell us about you as a person?
What was a common theme among the wishes?

"Weakness of attitude becomes weakness of character."
—Albert Einstein

SELF EXPLORATION ACTIVITIES

"You are the embodiment of the information you choose to accept and act upon. To change your circumstances you need to change your thinking and subsequent actions."—Adlin Sinclair

The purpose of self exploration activities is to have the participants in the small group learn about themselves and others through the themes, topics and questions related to each of the experiences. These activities provide an opportunity for the individuals to look at themselves in such a way that they begin to understand who they are as individuals, as members of a group, society and humanity. Hopefully through this process the individuals will also learn about others and their individual, group and societal goals, values and experiences.

Though self-exploration we learn how we fit in and how that understanding enables us to understand those around us. This includes family, friends, colleagues, supervisors and others. This knowledge and awareness will be helpful in the workplace, in school settings, community groups and in personal situations.

"A Face in the Crowd"

Goal: Participants will share personal information with each other in a one on one situation.

Directions: (1 hour)

Everyone will be split into two groups. Group A will stand in a circle, facing inward. Group B will stand in a circle outside of Group A, facing inward as well. When the music is played, Group B will walk around Group A. When the music stops, the people walking will stop as well. Group A will then turn around and face their partners for that round.

The facilitator will read a question out loud. The person in the inner circle is to answer the question. The person listening is allowed to ask questions in order to clarify what the person is saying but the focus must remain on the person answering the question.

After the round is over, the groups will reverse positions and repeat the exercise. This should be done for approximately six rounds.

Possible Questions for Exercise:

What is the biggest regret in your life? What makes that your biggest regret?
Tell me about a time you lost someone close to you? How did you deal with that situation?
What is one stereotype about your ethnicity that you dislike?
If you can make a movie about your life, what actor/actress would you cast? How come?
What to you is the most ultimate betrayal?
What would you want to improve about yourself, what would it be? How come?
What do you consider to be your greatest accomplishment so far? How come?
Tell me about a person you really admire?
Describe a difficult situation in your life. How did you deal with it?
Describe a time you lost trust in someone who is close to you?
What do you do when you feel unhappy?

After the questions have been asked, split the groups into smaller groups to begin the discussion portion of the exercise. Feel free to make your own set of questions for your group.

Small Group Facilitation Questions:

How did you feel about sharing intimate details of your life with a partner who you may or may not have known?
How did you feel about hearing intimate details of someone else's life who you may or may have not known?
What made you comfortable/uncomfortable about sharing?
How did you feel about the questions that were asked?
If you didn't have time to respond to your partner, how did that make you feel?

Large Group Facilitation Questions:

How did this activity affect you?
What did you think of this activity and what did you learn from it?

"All Alone"

Goal: During this exercise, the participants will be forced to spend "alone time" with themselves.

Directions: (1 hour and 30 minutes)

Split the larger group into smaller ones no larger than 8 per group. The facilitators will ask for everyone's phone, watches, mp3 players and all other devices.

For a given amount of time, the participants will be instructed to sit in silence with their eyes closed. They will not be able to talk, touch, or open their eyes for that time period. After time is up, the groups will discuss their experiences amongst themselves.

Small Group Facilitation Questions:

How did you feel about being alone?
How did you feel about having your communication devices taken away?
How did you spend the time?
What did you think about? How did it make you feel?
How long did you think you were alone for?
How many of you followed the instructions?
What made you comfortable or uncomfortable about being alone?
How is this different from when you choose to be alone?

Large Group Facilitation Questions:

What did you think of this exercise?
How did you feel not knowing what was going to happen next?
We were sitting in silence for ___ minutes. How long did it seem?

"Alternate Ending"

Goals: This activity prompts the participants to think about alternate life goals when their primary choices are taken away from them.

Materials: Index cards/pieces of paper and writing utensils.

Directions: (1 hour and 15 minutes)

Split the large group into groups of 6-8. Each participant should be given three index cards and a pencil. Each person is to write down three goals, each on a different index card. After writing the goals, have everyone share their goals with the group and what the goals mean to them. After sharing their goals with the group, everyone must rip up their most important goal . . . then their second . . . then their third.

(For more shock value, have the facilitators collect the cards and then proceed to rip them to shreds.)

Small group Facilitation Questions:

How did you feel about ripping up your most important goal?
How do you feel about ripping them *all* up?
What could get in the way of achieving your most important goal?
How would you feel about making new goals?
What would your new goals be?
What do you think about changing your mind about your goals?
What would happen if you achieved your ultimate goal?
What has happened in the past when a goal wasn't met?

Large Group Facilitation Questions:

How did you feel about this exercise?
How do you think you would change as a person if you could not accomplish your original goals?
How hard was it for you to think of new goals?

"Book of Life"

Goal: This activity allows for the participants to reflect on their lives by giving details about an imaginary autobiography they would write at the age of eighty five.

Direction: (1 hour and 15 minutes)

Split the large group into smaller ones. The facilitator will direct the participants as follows . . .

"Close your eyes and imagine that you have transported yourself through time to the point in your life where you are eighty five years old. Imagine you have written a book about yourself. Think about the title of the book. Think about the best times and the most difficult times. Take your time in doing so. When you have decided what these things will be, open your eyes.

Small Group Facilitation Questions:

What is the title of the book?
What made you pick this title?
What were the best parts?
What were the most difficult parts?
What does the book say about what you hope to attain?
How confident are you about your future?
What pages if any, would you burn?

Large Group Facilitation Questions:

How did you feel about fitting your life into one title?
If you could change your title, what would you change it to?
How did you feel about what other people shared in your group?
How did the thought of being 85 strike you?

"Card of Memories"

Goal: The object of this activity is to facilitate group sharing of personal ideas and feelings through a simple card memorization game.

Materials: 24 index cards per group

Direction: (1 hour and 30 minutes)

Split the large group into groups of 6-8. 24 cards will be placed face down. Each has a word or phrase written on the other side. (For example: Dreams, Most Embarrassing Moment, Anxiety, Depression, Love)

The object of the game is to match each card with its partner card, which has the same word. When someone flips over two cards that do not match, the person should talk about how the words relate to each other for themselves specifically.

The cards should be put back in the same place facing down. The next person will then proceed to attempt to match two cards, keeping in mind the cards that were turned over beforehand. It is *literally* a game of memory in multiple ways.

If the two cards are matched, then the person who picked them will talk about the word or phrase that is written on the card and what it means to him/her. Once that person is finished speaking, the group may address the word, ask the person questions and go into brief discussions about it. Once that is done, the next person continues the process.

*It is imperative that the facilitators prevent any discussions from running too long in order to ensure that everyone has a chance of sharing.

Small Group Facilitation Questions:

How did you feel about sharing your personal experiences with the group?
What word would you have liked to be in the game or what word would you have liked to talk about?
How did you feel talking about the positives and negatives at the same time?
What was it like to listen to your peers share their stories?

Large Group Facilitation Questions:

What did you like about the Memory game?
As a group what did you find common in your experiences? What was different?

"Changes Within"

Goals: This activity allows the participants to temporarily possess a trait they wish they already had. It also allows them to understand how they portray themselves to others and how others perceive them.

Directions: (1 hour and 15 minutes)

Split the larger group into smaller groups. The participants will think of a trait that they would like to have. They will not share this trait with other members of the group. They will act out the trait and talk with members of the group as that trait, by answering questions in the manner of the trait. Each person in the group will take turns asking the participant questions in order to guess the trait.

Each person in the group will secretly guess what the trait is and after everyone has had a turn asking questions, the group members will begin revealing what their guesses were. Each member will explain what made them guess that trait by giving specific examples.

The participant will then reveal what the trait was. After everyone has had a chance at revealing their traits, the discussions will begin.

Small Group Facilitation Questions:

What suggestions do you have to help the participant express the desired trait better?
What effect do you think your trait has on your interpersonal skills?
How can you apply these remarks from the group to anything that will help you to be successful in acquiring this trait?

Large Group Facilitation Questions:

How did this activity make you feel?
What have you learned from this experience?

Where will you be using the trait, now that you have received feedback from the group?

"Coat of Arms"

Goal: This activity is designed to allow participants to reveal how they view themselves and their families and what is important to them, through symbols.

Materials: Writing utensils and drawing paper

Directions: (45 minutes to an hour)

A coat of arms originated in the mid 12 century first used by feudal lords and knights. It is an arrangement of symbols or words, usually depicted on and around a shield that indicates ancestry and distinctions. Each design is unique to a person, family, corporation, or state.

A brief synopsis on the history and usages of "Coats of Arms" should be given to the group in case participants aren't sure what it and its purpose is. Each participant will be given a writing utensil and a sheet of paper, preferably with a blank shield on it. The facilitator should ask the group . . .

What is your "Coat of Arms"?
What represents you as an individual?
How are you symbolic in your society?
What is important to you in this world?
What is important to your family in this world?

The individuals should begin to draw the "Coat of Arms" on the paper provided. After this is done, each participant will introduce himself/herself and tell the group about their "Coat of Arms".

Large Group Facilitation Questions:

How did you feel about this exercise?
How did you feel about sharing this representation of you?
Has your coat always been the same? Do you see it changing? Has it changed in the past year?
What made you choose this representation?
If given a larger crest what would you put on it?

"Cycles of Life"

Goal: To allow the participants to introduce themselves by explaining their current life cycle.

Materials: Drawing paper and drawing utensils

Directions: (1 hour)

Everyone goes through various cycles in their lives. Have the group members think of a particular cycle in their lives that they feel they are in as of now. In other words, what is a reoccurring concept or event in their lives? The cycles can range from mental, emotional, physical, spiritual, or any combination of these.

The facilitator should instruct everyone to draw or write down the cycle in their lives that they find themselves in. After this is done, the participants will then introduce themselves by explaining the cycle to the rest of the group. Depending on the size of the group, time should be allocated accordingly.

Large Group Facilitation Question:

How do you feel about this exercise?
What did you learn about your cycle?
What thoughts came to mind during this exercise?

If you had the chance to do this activity over, how do you think your cycle may have been different?
What did you learn about the others in your group?

"The Genie & Me"

Goal: This activity allows the participants to reveal their future goals and methods they plan on achieving them. The personal relationship to the future goal is examined as well.

Directions: (1 hour and 15 minutes)

Split the larger group in smaller ones. The facilitators will announce to the group that . . .

"While driving through your neighborhood, a Genie's car broke down and you were kind enough to assist him/her. The Genie was extremely grateful for your assistance because, as we all know; Genies don't know anything about cars. For your kind efforts, the Genie will give you three wishes that will bring you closer to achieving your future goal/s".

"The wishes granted will not complete the goals but only assist you in your journey towards it. However, the Genie can only grant these wishes if you know what these future goals are"

Small Group Facilitation Questions:

What would you wish for?
What is your future goal/s?
How do you feel about discussing your future?
How did you feel about getting wishes to help you attain your goals?
How would you feel if you were handed your goal?
How do you feel about your future?
What would you do if your goals were not attainable?

Large Group Facilitation Questions:

How did you feel about sharing your future?
How did you feel about talking about your goals?
How come the Genie only offered to assist you in attaining your goals instead of just giving it to you?
What are your feelings about your future now that you've talked about it?

"Great Escape"

Goal: This activity will focus on the desire or need to escape from the realities of our daily lives.

Directions: (1 hour and 15 minutes)

Split the large group into groups of 6-8. The facilitator will instruct the participants to imagine they are escaping from reality. Where would you go? Each question should be answered with this in mind.

Give the participants a few minutes to visualize their place of escape. While the participants are visualizing, the facilitator should ask the *"Small Group Facilitation Questions"*, in order to give the participants an idea of what they should be thinking about while visualizing an escape. When visualizing time is over, the facilitator can proceed with the questions.

Small Group Facilitation Questions:

What are you escaping from? How come?
What are you trying to leave behind, as opposed to going towards?
What would be comforting for you to have with you?
How would you pass your time if you escaped?
What would you hope to find?

How would your escape benefit you?
How long would you escape for?

Large Group Facilitation Questions:

What in your life do you need to escape from?
When you go back to your reality, what would be different? How would you approach things? Would it be the same or different?

"Guess Who"

Goal: To allow the participants to reveal facts about themselves that aren't known by many people.

Materials: Index card and writing utensils

Directions: (1 hour and 15 minutes)

Split the large group into groups of 6-8. Each person will be given an index card and a pen. On the index card they are to write down a fact about themselves that many people do not know. After this is done, they are to hand the card to the facilitator, who will then shuffle and redistribute them. Each person will get to ask 3 questions regarding the fact.

For example, if the fact is "I was a ballet dancer", someone may ask "Who likes to perform?", "Who likes classical music?" etc.

Small Group Facilitation Questions:

What types of things did you learn about your group members that surprised you?
What didn't surprise you?
Tell us any follow up questions you may have regarding the facts you learned about your group members.

Large Group Facilitation Questions:

How did you feel about sharing secrets with the people in your group? What were your reasons for choosing the fact you disclosed?

"Guided Imagery"

Goal: This activity allows the participants to acknowledge and share what fame and notoriety would mean and how it would feel to them.

Directions: (45 minutes to an hour)

Split everyone up into smaller groups, no larger than 8 per group. Have the group members sit in a small circle. Instruct everyone to close their eyes. A facilitator will lead the **entire** group through this story.

"Red Carpet/Awards Ceremony" (the story should be embellished where ever the facilitator sees fit but the core storyline must remain prevalent.)

:: Limo ride to ceremony with your date—walking up red carpet surrounded by screaming fans—interview on red carpet—through the doors and escorted to seat—reading nominations—you win!—you are given 15 seconds to make a speech/give thanks—you are led off stage:

Ideas for follow up questions: (Select questions for the smaller groups and the entire group.)

Who did you take to the ceremony? Explain
How did you feel traveling to the ceremony? (excited, calm, anxious)
What were you and your date wearing? (fashionable, formal, casual, grungy, conservative)

What was it like to have hundreds of screaming fans wanting you to notice them? (exhilarating, scary, confusing)
What did the interviewer ask you?
How did you feel being the center of attention?
What, if anything did you expect to see behind the doors before entering the ceremony? What did you actually see?
How close/far did you sit from the stage?
What was the first thing you thought when they announced you as the winner?
What emotions did you feel when they announced you as the winner?
What did you say in your 15 second speech?
How did it feel to be led offstage to make room for the next winner?

Large Group Facilitation Question:

What did this fantasy tell you about yourself and others?

"Headband Exercise"

Goal: This activity allows the participants to become aware of their actions in regards to how they are treated by those around them

Materials: Headbands/index cards and tape.

Directions: (1 hour and 15 minutes)

Everyone will be given a headband with a phrase written on it. (If headbands are not available, it can be an index card that can be safely attached to the participant's forehead. Everyone should be instructed to not look at what is written on the headbands they receive.

The phrases or attributes that are to be written can vary as the facilitator sees fit. However, here are a few examples of possible selections . . .

Example: Outcast, Popular, Respected, Well-known, Nerd, Big Man On Campus, etc

Split the group into smaller ones and everyone should mingle with others in the group. However, the participants are required to treat each other as their headband dictates. This should go on for ten minutes or so.

Small Group Facilitation Questions:

How did you feel about this exercise?
What were some of the problems of trying to be yourself while others were treating you differently?
How did you act differently as the mingling continued based on the way you were being treated? If so, how did you behave?
Did anyone find themselves being treated in a way they've never been treated? How did it feel?
If you could switch headbands/tags with someone in your group, which one would it be? How come?
If you were given a blank card what would you write? How come?
In what situations have you had to change your behavior in order to accommodate someone else?
When have there been times where you've needed to change your behavior but didn't?

Large Group Facilitation Questions:

How did it feel to have to change yourself in order to mingle with the others in the group?
How did you change as the mingling continued?
How similar or different are you from your headband role?

"Hot Seat"

Goal: This activity is a very direct way to prompt participants to share about their personal lives by putting them on the "hot seat". They are at the mercy of their group members and the questions that will be hurled towards them.

Materials: Envelopes and index cards with questions written on them.

Directions: (1 hour and 15 minutes)

Split the larger group into groups of 6-8. The facilitator will distribute envelopes to each member of the group. Inside each envelope there will be an index card with a personal question. No one is allowed to look inside the envelope until they are in the hot seat.

The person who is first on the hot seat is determined by the facilitator, by tossing a soft ball to a member of the group. (Any soft object that lacks sharp edges will do. A trip to the emergency room is not an intended part of this exercise.)

Then that member will toss the ball to another member of the group which will determine the next person to be in the hot seat. This must go on until every group member has been in the hot seat.

The person in the hot seat is to answer the question as thoroughly and honestly as possible. Then members of the group will be given a chance to ask the person in the hot seat follow up questions based on the response of the person in the hot seat.

Questions/Situations Printed on Cards for Hot Seat:

What is your biggest fear about your future? How might your fear become reality?

Whom do you trust the most in your life? What makes this person different from everyone else?
What is something that people may be surprised to learn about you?
What is your most prized possession? What about it makes it so important to you?
You are about to have your first child. Where are you in your life?
If you could relive one moment or time in your life what would it be?
If you could change one thing about yourself or your life what would it be?

Small Group Facilitation Questions:

How did it feel being in the hot seat?
How did it feel asking questions to the person in the hot seat?
What other questions would you have asked if you would ask more than one to each person?
What situation would you have liked to have and why?
What is your favorite situation and which was your least favorite?

Large Group Facilitation Questions:

What new information did you learn about someone in your group?
What other situations would you have wanted?
How did your answers reflect your ideals and dreams?

"I Want to. I Wouldn't Dare."

Goal: This is an opportunity for the participants to look within themselves and communicate authentically with the group.

Directions: (1 hour)

This activity can work as an opening activity as well, depending on what personal information the participants are willing to divulge to the group. There are two ways of conducting this . . .

Opening Activity Method: If the group is still attempting to get comfortable with each other, gather the entire group in the form of a circle. The facilitator will then ask the group two questions and give them a few minutes to think about their answers.

Question 1: What is one thing you would want to do, that you haven't already done?

Question 2: What is one thing you would want to do, that you would never dare do?

Everyone should answer in the response form *"I want to . . ."* and *"I wouldn't dare . . ."* If time permits, the facilitator can ask "how come?" after everyone's answered the questions.

Self Explorations Method: This method is most effective when the group has begun to open up to each other. The facilitator can set the trend of openness by answering the questions first. This is an opportunity for the participants to look within themselves and communicate authentically with the group.

To allow an in depth look at each participant, the facilitator should split the group into smaller ones. After the members in the smaller groups have answered the questions, the facilitators and fellow group members can ask follow up questions within their respective groups.

Small Group Facilitation Questions:

How come?
What do you think your answers say about your overall character?
How do you feel about your answers?
What did you learn about yourself through this exercise?
What did you learn about your group members through this exercise?

Large Group Facilitation Questions:

What did you learn about yourself through this exercise?
How has this activity changed the way you view things?

"If I Had a Million Dollars"

Goal: This activity allows the participants to examine their actions and thought process when confronted with the notion of receiving a large sum of money.

Directions: (1 hour and 15 minutes)

Split everyone into groups no larger than 8. Announce that each team has inherited a million dollars USD. It helps to hand out fake cash, a check or something tangible because this helps simulate the reality of receiving a gift.

There are three rules for them to follow once they receive the money.

- The group cannot split the money.
- The money used must benefit the group.
- If you choose to spend the money on yourself, it has to be agreed upon by the group. (General consensus can come from a democratic voting process, heads or tails, rock paper scissors, or an old fashioned roman Greco wrestling match. The method is up to the team. Just get it done.

Once it has been decided (or not decided) what to do with the money, the facilitators will ask the following questions . . .

Small Group Facilitation Questions:

How did you feel as a group about how you spent the money?

How did you feel about trusting in other people that the money would be used in good ways?
Who do you think was causing the conflict, if any? How come?
When in your life have you had to work within a group to make a decision?

Large Group Facilitation Questions:

What did your group decide to do with the money?
What did you learn about yourself during this exercise?
What did you learn about others?
What did you like or dislike about the small groups and how things were handled in them?
What would you do if you were alone in this exercise?

"Inside Out"

Goal: In this exercise, everyone will be asked to reveal something about themselves that others in the group may not know about them.

Materials: Writing utensils and paper.

Directions: (1 hour and 15 minutes)

Split the large group into smaller ones. Everyone is to write on a card/piece of paper, an emotion, act or something that you do that others in the group do not know. When everyone has written something down, they will place it in a basket where they can and will be shuffled around.

After deciding who goes first, everyone picks one card from the container. Each person reads it aloud and says the name of who they believe wrote the card. The facilitator will write down the name of the person guessing and the name they guessed. When all of the names have been written, the facilitator will go back to the first person and say "Please repeat what you said and who you chose." Whether they guess correctly or not, the person who did write on the card will explain their reason for sharing this emotion/act. The facilitator will wait until everyone has had a chance to speak before asking everyone to reveal what they wrote down.

Small Group Facilitation Questions:

How do you feel about revealing this?
What prevents you from showing it to others?

Large Group Facilitation Questions:

How do you feel about revealing something about yourself to those who might not realize this is in you?
How do you feel now that people know this about you?

"Jekyll & Hyde"

Goal: Each person will be asked to think about the various masks that they wear in different situations. They will be asked to discuss how they feel about them and how they deal with them

Directions: (1 hour and 30 minutes)

Split the large group into smaller groups. The facilitator will begin the activity by reading this quote . . .

"In each of us, two natures are at war—the good and the evil. All our lives the fight goes on between them, and one of them must conquer. But in our own hands lies the power to choose—what we want most to be, we are."—Anonymous

With the quotation in mind, the participants should ***think*** about . . .

What masks do you wear in different situations?
How do you feel about them?
How do you deal with them?
How do you think others view your masks?

Small Group Facilitation Questions:

How do you see yourself?
How do you think others see you?
How do you want to be seen?
What types of masks do you wear in different situations?
Which mask would you want to get rid of or change?
Which masks do you like the most or least?
What are your fears about revealing what your masks are?
In what situations do your masks conflict?
How do you feel, now that your masks are revealed?
Are there other masks that you still have? What has stopped you from revealing these?

Large Group Facilitation Questions:

What did you learn about yourself?
How did you feel talking about yourself?
What did you learn about others?

"Last Chance"

Goal: To allow participants to consider saying what they never could to a loved one.

Directions: (1 hour and 15 minutes)

Split the large group into groups of 6-8. The facilitator should direct the group with this passage . . .

"You're standing alone in your apartment. Your bags stand packed against the wall near the door. Its finally hitting you that you're leaving—never again to see your family, friends or anyone you're acquainted with. You look around at the bare floors and walls, trying to remember anything you've forgotten. You've said your "goodbyes" and you're resigned to the fact that you must leave. It's now or never! You've got to do it. There's something you must say to someone that you couldn't say when you said "goodbye". You pick up the phone . . ."

Small Group Facilitation Questions:

Who is this person and what do you need to say?
How would you like this person to respond? How do you think they will respond?
What has kept you from telling the person this in the past?
How would you feel if you were to go away without telling that person?
Under what circumstances would you be able to say this to the person?

Large Group Facilitation Questions:

How did you feel sharing this issue with a group when you haven't been able to share it with that person?
How did the issues people brought up effect the way in which the group interacted?
Now that you've shared this with your group, will this make it easier to confront that person?
What else would you like to say?

"Life's Successes"

Goals: This activity allows participants to discuss happiness, prosperity and success in their respective life goals.

Directions: (1 hour)

Split the large group into smaller ones.

Small Group Facilitation Questions:

What does success and happiness mean to you?
What in life makes you happy or makes you feel successful?
What does achieving success/prosperity mean to you?
When in your life have you been most productive? How did this happen?
What is missing from your life that could make you feel happy and prosperous?
When in life have you needed to look for happiness?
When do you think "enough is enough" in terms of achieving success?

Large Group Facilitation Questions:

How did it feel to share your feelings of success and happiness with others?
How do you feel about your definition of success and happiness after hearing everyone in your group share their definition?

"Mirror and Me"

Goal: This activity allows participants to reveal to the group how they perceive themselves and how they *wish* to perceive themselves, inwardly and outwardly.

Materials: Several Mirrors

Directions: (1 hour and 15 minutes)

Split the larger group into groups of 6-8. Hand every facilitator in the groups a mirror. Each participant in the group will look in the mirror and share with the group what they see in themselves.

Since this is a rather personal activity and tensions may be high at the beginning of this, the facilitator can be the first to share. Another benefit of the facilitator sharing first is that he/she will be able to help set the tone of how deep or superficial the group may go with such an exercise.

Small Group Facilitation Questions:

What do you see when you look in the mirror?
What do you think others see? How come?
How would you like to be viewed?
How important to you is it how others view you?
How has your view of yourself changed over the years?
How important is physical appearance to you?
When have you found someone's physical appearance intimidating?
If there was one physical thing you would change about yourself, what would it be?
How do you treat people based upon appearance?
How do views of yourself affect your relationship with others?
What did you wish you would have revealed? How come?
What do you wish you wouldn't have revealed? How come?
How were you affected by the things said by members of the group?

Large Group Facilitation Questions:

How did it feel to share such personal information to the group? How come?
On a scale of 1-10, how open were you with your communication with your group? How come?

How did it feel to discuss issues of physicality with others? How come?

What else would you have liked to discuss that you didn't get a chance to?

"My New Neighbor"

Goals: The participants will be given the opportunity to compare what they believe to be their best qualities to what other people believe are their best qualities.

Directions: (1 hour and 15 minutes)

Hopefully by this time in the program, the participants have gotten to know each other. This activity works better if the participants have spent a weekend together or have prior knowledge of each other and aren't complete strangers.

Material: Paper and writing utensils

Everyone should sit in a circle and be given a piece of paper. On one side, they are to write their names and on the other side, they should write what they believe their best quality to be.

The facilitators should prepare a container filled with the names of all the participants. Each participant should come up to the container and pick out a name that isn't their own. On the blank side of that paper they have selected, they are to write the name of the person they picked and what they believe is that person's best quality.

The facilitator will begin by calling on someone to read the name of the person they chose from the container, and what they said was that person's best quality. The person who was described then reads their own quality they wrote about themselves, and sits next to the person who called their name, therefore, becoming their new neighbor.

When everyone has been arranged in a new circle, the facilitators may ask questions if time permits.

Small Group Facilitation Questions:

How did it feel to let the group know what you considered your best quality?
How easy was it for you to think of qualities of yourself and the other person?
How do you feel about what someone else said about you?

Large Group Facilitation Questions:

How did you feel when you heard what someone thought was your best quality? How well did it match what you had for yourself?
If there was no match, how do you think the other person formed that idea of you? When have you heard that about yourself before?
How do people's best qualities show in their daily activities?

"Past Experience"

Goal: All human beings have a past, which makes them who they are today. In the following exercise, we will discuss different aspects of your pasts.

Directions: (1 hour and 15 minutes)

Split the large group into groups of 6-8. The facilitator should instruct the participants to take a moment to reflect on the different experiences that they have encountered throughout their lives that have influenced who they are today.

Small Group Facilitation Questions:

If you could relive a time in your life, what would it be?
How would you describe that time? Was it a positive or negative time? How come?
What made you choose this experience?
If you could change anything about it, what would it be?

Large Group Facilitation Questions:

How did you feel about completing this exercise?
How did you feel about discussing your past with your group?

"Personal Ads"

Goal: This activity allows the participants to discuss what they look for in a significant other. The qualities they are in search of will give insight into the character traits of the participant.

Directions: (1 hour)

Split the large group into smaller ones. The facilitator should instruct the participants to think about the qualities they would want their significant other to possess. They should also think about why they would want these certain attributes in a partner and what does it say about them for wanting this?

After everyone has presented their personal ad, the facilitator can begin asking deeper questions.

Small Group Facilitation Questions:

What makes those qualities/attributes so important to you?
What do you feel you need from your significant other?
Where are these qualities now in your life?

Are these qualities wants or requirements?

Large Group Facilitation Questions:

How did it feel to reveal such information to the group?
How willing are you to alter your requirements/wants?

"Personal Pyramid"

Goals: The pyramid should reflect what a person feels are their building blocks of life, meaning their priorities and values.

Materials: Drawing paper and writing utensils.

Directions: (1 hour)

Split the larger group in smaller ones. Instruct the participants to create a pyramid on a sheet of paper. The pyramid will be made out of six separate blocks. Three on the bottom row, two in the middle, and one on the top.

There are 12 "building blocks" to choose from: Family, Friends, Religion, Culture, Education, Career, Money, Marriage, Ethnicity, Gender roles, Sexual Orientation.

(The participants are allowed to come up with three categories of their own if it is not listed above.)

Each participant will show the pyramid they've made to their respective groups. There should be a brief question and answer period for two to three minutes after this. These questions should be asked by group members but the facilitators can lead discussions if the group is dragging along.

Small Group Facilitation Questions:

What made you leave out the other blocks?
What made these specific building blocks important to you?
What made you decide to place the blocks the way you did?

Large Group Facilitation Questions:

How did you feel about discussing your priorities and values?

"Pictures and Goals"

Goals: To allow participants to think about their desired goals and focus on what they are doing to obtain these desired things.

Materials: Various pictures (pre cut) from different magazines, construction paper and glue.

Directions: (1 hour and 30 minutes)

Split the participants into smaller groups. Each person will receive a piece of construction paper. Each person is instructed to choose 3 pictures from the center of the table, that represents a desired goal or achievement of theirs, and paste it onto their sheet. After everyone is done, have everyone share what they chose.

Small Group Facilitation Questions:

What made you pick these pictures?
What do they mean to you?
How does it feel to have these pictures (desired goals/achievements) in front of you?
Did you get the picture(s) you wanted? If not, how did it feel not to get it?
What pictures would you have liked?

Large Group Facilitation Questions:

Who wants to share the kinds of pictures they picked?
How did you feel about the pictures? How come?

"Pieces of Me"

Goal: The purpose of this activity is to (1) Share spontaneous memories amongst a small group. (2) Bring people back to memories of the past and acknowledge how these events in their lives play a role, if any, on who they are today.

Materials: Random items such as jacks, dice, keys, shells, matches, candy, buttons, pen/marker, change (quarter or dime), music related items, or nature related objects. (These are just a few possible ideas)

Directions: (1 hour and 15 minutes)

Split the large group into smaller groups of 6-8. Have everyone in the groups sit in a circle. The facilitator will hand the bag to the participants. The participants should choose an item that BEST suits a memory or interest of theirs. Each participant MUST choose one item. No items can be exchanged between members of the group, or with the bag if a person notices an item they would have rather picked, if it has passed their turn

The bags of items for each group will be pre-packaged at random. The groups will have similar items. After everyone has picked an item, the bag should be placed in the middle of the circle. Each member is encouraged to explain in what way their item relates to themselves.

Small Group Facilitation Questions:

How did you feel about this "forced choice" exercise?
What other items would you liked to have seen in the bag?
If your item was not your first choice, which one would have been? How come?
How do you feel about sharing your personal memories with the group?
In what other situations have you been forced to make a choice?
How do you feel about being forced to make choices?

Large Group Facilitation Questions:

What do you feel is the main goal of this exercise?
How does it relate to how you live your life?

"Rituals"

Goal: This activity allows participants to examine the social roles they play in their communities as well as the rituals they partake in.

Directions: (1 hour and 15 minutes)

Split the larger group into smaller groups of 6-8 participants. Facilitators will give out passages from *Body Rituals performed by the Nacirema*. Each group will have the same passage. The facilitators will read the passage out loud to the group.

Passage: "There remains one other kind of practitioner, known as the "listener". This witch doctor has the power to exorcise the devils that lodge in the heads of people who have been bewitched. The Nacirema believe that parents bewitch their own children. Mothers are particularly suspected of putting a curse on children while teaching them the secret rituals. The counter-magic of the witch doctor is unusual in its lack of ritual. The patient simply tells the "listener" all his/her troubles and fears; beginning with the earliest difficulties he can remember. The memory displayed by the Nacirema in these exorcism sessions is truly remarkable. It is not uncommon for the patient to bemoan the rejection he felt upon being weaned as a babe, and a few Individuals even see their troubles going back to traumatic effects of their own birth"

After everyone has finished, facilitators can use the following questions to guide the discussion.

Small Group Facilitation Questions:

In the passage, we learned that the Nacirema people go to the witch doctor when they need someone to listen to their problems. Who is the listener in your life? (Who do you go to when you need to talk to someone?)

What does the word "ritual" mean to you?
Think about the roles that we play in our work, social, and personal lives. What are some of the rituals that you participate in because of your role?
What are some rituals that make you feel part of the group? What are some rituals that can exclude other people from a group?

Large Group Facilitation Questions:

What did your group get out of the passage?
What were some of the rituals that came up in your group?

"Rolling on a Fear"

Goal: This activity allows participants to explore one another's fears as well as sharing them with others. However, this isn't the venue to try to solve the fears.

Let The Games Begin

Materials: Dice with different categories written on each side. Possible categories can be friendship, relationships, family, school, or career.

Directions: (1 hour)

Split the large group into groups of 6-8. Each person takes turns rolling the dice. Whichever category the person lands on, they must speak of a fear/hesitation related to that topic.

After everyone discusses a fear, the group can now ask questions about each other's fears. When everyone feels they have explored enough, they can continue to roll the dice again and explore fears in other areas.

Small Group Facilitation Questions: (Optional)

How do you feel about exposing that fear to the group?
Who else have you mentioned this fear to?
When have you faced this fear in the past?
What does this fear prevent you from doing?
Whose fear can you relate to, if any? How?
How can you overcome this fear?

Large Group Facilitation Question:

How did this activity make you feel?
What feelings of discomfort, if any, did this activity evoke?
What impact did hearing others fears have on you?
What did you learn about yourself?

"Spin the Bottle"

Goals: This activity prompts the participants to answer personal questions when asked at random, in front of a small group.

Materials: A bottle and a list of various questions.

Directions: (1 hour)

Split the large group into smaller ones. The facilitators should have everyone sit in a circle and then place a bottle in the middle of the circle. This activity functions just as the classic game of "spin the bottle" works. However, the kisses are replaced with questions. Whichever two people the bottle lands on will have the opportunity to ask each other a question from a list created by the facilitators.

Depending on the level of comfort with the group, the questions can be more personal or superficial. However this activity works much better if there have been prior deep levels of sharing and communication between the participants.

Sample Questions:

Tell us about a conflict you had in your life.
What do you think are positive challenges? How come?
What are some risks you have taken and what were the consequences?
When in your life have you wanted to start over again? How come?
What types of things make you feel overwhelmed? How come?
What stresses you out the most? How come?
What image do you feel you have to live up to? How come?
How important is it to you how others perceive you? How come?
Where does your biggest sense of joy stem from? How come?
If you could exchange lives with someone, who would it be? How come?
What past experiences have made you trustful or guarded towards the opposite sex? How come?
What would you like to change in the way others perceive you? How come?
Describe yourself.

After everyone has had a chance to answer more than once, the facilitation questions can begin.

Small Group Facilitation Questions:

How did it feel to share with the group in this manner?
What question would you have wanted to answer?
What question would you have liked to ask someone else?

Large Group Facilitation Questions:

What do you think the purpose of this activity was?
How easy was it to answer the questions honestly?

"Taking Sides"

Goal: This activity allows participants to deal with everyday conflicts in one's life and see how they respond within the situation.

Materials: Envelopes and cards with scenarios written on them

Directions: (1 Hour and 30 minutes)

Split the large group into separate groups. The facilitator will inform the participants that they are trapped in a character other than their own. Each of them will be paired off, and then instructed to pick a scenario from the envelope. They will be given 3-5 minutes to act it out. After every group has gone, the facilitation questions will begin.

Examples of scenarios used: Parent/child—career choice, friends spreading rumors, significant other cheating, friends breaking promises etc.

Small Group Facilitation Questions:

How close to home were certain scenarios for you?
What motivated you to play the role the way you did?
If you had a chance, would you deal with certain situations differently? How so?
In any of the conflicts, would you take a certain side? How come?

Large Group Facilitation Questions:

1) How did you feel being in a spontaneous conflict situation? How come?
2) How did it feel watching others deal with certain conflict situations?

"Things We've Lost"

Goals: This activity allows the participants to share with their group members things they have lost in life and discuss how it has impacted them.

Materials: Index cards and a paper bag.

Directions: (1 hour and 30 minutes)

Split the large group into smaller ones. Each group will be given a small paper bag filled with index cards. On each index card is a different loss written down. Each participant is to pick a card out of the bag. If the person has a connection to the loss, they are to speak about it. If they do not have a connection to it, they are to choose another card.

Ideas for losses written on cards: morals & values, family member, money, love, significant other, mind, friend, opportunity, pet, innocence, something sentimental, financial, career.

Small Group Facilitation Questions:

How long ago have you lost this?
How has this loss impacted your life?
How did you react right after this loss?
How did you feel when you realized it was lost?
How would life be different if you still had it?
Who have you shared this loss with?
What has made this loss easier for you?
What good has come out of this loss?
How do you think you can find or come close to regaining what you have lost?

Large Group Facilitation Questions:

How did it feel sharing your loss?
How did it feel to hear about others losses?
What have you learned from expressing this loss?

"Wall Around Our Heart"

Goals: This activity explores the emotional defense systems of the participants

Directions: (1 hour and 30 minutes)

Split the group into smaller ones. The facilitator will direct the groups in what to do now . . .

"Visualize your heart. What does it look like? How is it shaped? What color is it? What size is it? Your heart can look like anything. Use your imagination. (i.e. Valentine, biological heart, ball etc.)

"Now remember back to your past. Remember a time when you experienced emotional hurt. What brought it on? What or who caused it? What do you remember about the incident? Remember what you felt along with that pain. What did you do? What didn't you do? Just go deep within yourself."

"Now envision a wall around your heart. What does it look like? What is it made of? How big is it? What shape is it? What color is it? Look behind that wall. What do you see? Who do you see? What are you doing behind this wall?

"Envision your heart again."

Small Group Facilitation Question: (the questions should be used to facilitate the conversation. Answering ALL of the questions is not required for the exercise's success)

What did your heart look like?
What do the characteristics of the heart represent?
How far back did you remember?
What was the incident that caused you the pain?
What were you feeling along with this pain?
How did you react? What did you do? What didn't you do?
What would you have done differently after knowing what you know now?
What would your heart look like if you had done things differently?
What did the wall look like? What function does it have?
What does that represent for you?
If you didn't have this wall around your heart, what would your heart look like?
Do you hide behind that wall today?
What are you doing behind this wall?

Large Group Facilitation Questions:

How did you feel about the exercise?
How comfortable were you with the people in your group?
Who else's heart looked like yours?

After looking behind your wall, how strong is it now as opposed to before?
How vulnerable do you become when people see what is behind the wall?

"War"

Goal: There are many things that come from the realities of war. The biggest tends to be loss. Others could be separation and unity. The following activity explores the loss, separation and unification that all of us have gone through in life. Perhaps everyone hasn't been in an actual "war" but we all have fought our own wars in everyday life.

Directions: (1 hour and 15 minutes)

Split the large group into smaller groups of 6-8 participants.

Small Group Facilitation Questions:

When you hear the word "loss" what comes to mind?
If you could get someone or something back that you've lost, what would it be? How come?
To what extent would you go to in order to prevent the loss of someone you love?
How have you dealt with the loss of someone/thing important to you?
How have/would you help a friend or relative who has recently suffered a loss?
When in your life have you been involved in someone else's war? How did you feel?
What type of separation have you experienced?
What family experience has unified your family the most?

Large Group Facilitation Questions:

How did you feel about sharing your losses with others in your group?
How did you feel when you heard about the losses of others?

"Wheel of Reflections"

Goal: To allow participants the opportunity to share how they feel about a specific topic and how it related to them in the past, present and how it may affect their future.

Materials: A pre cut wheel with a spinner attached to the center, with specific categories listed within it.

Possible categories: Loyalty, friends, family, recognition, pleasure, wisdom, conflict, achievements, autonomy, wealth, power, love, partner, physical appearance, health, skill/work, emotional well being, knowledge, morality or religion/faith.

Directions: (1 hour and 45 minutes)

Split the participants into smaller groups. Each group will be given a wheel and each person will be given a chance to spin the wheel or the spinner. After it lands on a category, the facilitator will begin asking the questions.

Small Group Facilitation Questions:

What is the most positive thing about this?
What is the most negative thing about this?
What types of experience(s) have you had with ____?
How has/is ____ affecting you?
How do you see ____ affecting you in the future?

Tell us about ____ in an instance where it has really affected you.
What caused these feelings?
How does ____ relate to you?
What category would you have liked to see on the wheel?

Large Group Facilitation Questions:

1) How do you feel about talking about these topics and emotions towards them?

"Where Do I Belong?"

Goal: To facilitate the discussion of being judged by appearances.

Directions: (1 hour)

The facilitators will announce that they are going to pick people for the next exercise. Then they will quietly choose people that they want in their group based on some unsaid criteria (which will based solely on appearance). The groups should range from 8 to 10 people. The facilitators will tap the people they want on the shoulder and indicate where they want them to go. When everyone is in their groups, the facilitation questions will be discussed within the smaller groups.

Small Group Facilitation Questions:

What is it about yourself that makes you belong to this group?
What is it about yourself that makes you feel alienated from this group? (After this question is answered, the facilitator should tell the group members why they were picked.)
How does it feel to be labeled based on a certain physical characteristic?
Where have you seen this sort of selection in everyday situations?
Where have you seen this in different cultures? Within what cultures?

When is it acceptable to choose people based on appearances?

Large Group Facilitation Questions:

How did the facilitators feel about picking certain people and not others?
When asked, who figured out the real reason they were picked to be in the group? What were other theories?
What are some of your thoughts and feelings after the reason was revealed to you?
What do you think this activity was meant to demonstrate?

"Courage doesn't always roar. Sometimes it is the quiet voice at the end of the day saying, "I will try again tomorrow."
—Mary Anne Radmacher

TEAM BUILDING

"Time goes by so fast, people go in and out of your life. You must never miss the opportunity to tell these people how much they mean to you."—Anonymous

Team building activities allow participants the opportunity to work with others in trying to achieve a common goal. More importantly, it allows the participants to reflect on their actions and role(s) within the group at the present time and compare it to their role(s) in the past. Through self and group analysis, the participants can identify what type of teammate they would like to be and begin to work towards this. Of course, the role of an individual is subject to change, depending on the group he/she is in but hopefully these activities will help the participants to be more flexible and open to a variety of experiences.

No matter where a person goes, they will always be a member of a team. Teams are found everywhere; in a family, at work, in a collegiate or religious institutions, sports teams, friendships or even an angry mob! Humans are social creatures by nature and that means we're going to be around each other, often. So we might as well learn how to *play well with others*.

"Balloon Toss"

Goal: To allow group members to work and communicate together in an effort to achieve a common goal of juggling toss.

Materials: Balloons

Direction: (30-45 minutes)

Split the large group into smaller ones and have them stand in a circle. The facilitator will toss balloons, one at a time; until all the balloons have been tossed in. (The number of balloons tossed in will depend on the size of the group or the facilitator's desire to make the activity more challenging.)

The group must keep each of the balloons in the air, but no one can touch the same balloon twice in a row. If they do, they are eliminated for that round and must stand aside and watch their team compete shorthanded.

After the first round is complete, the facilitator will tell different participants what body part they cannot use to touch the balloon. No one is allowed to touch the balloon twice in a row.

The rounds can continue in this fashion, becoming more challenging or the activity can be ended there. However, a lovely way to spice things up is by adding a competitive edge to this exercise. Teams can compete against each other in order to see who the supreme "Balloon Tossers" are. Each round of competition can increase with difficulty by adding more restrictions and adding more balloons into the mix.

Large Group Facilitation Questions:

1) How well did you work with the people in your group?
2) How did it feel to be part of a team?

3) How did it feel to be limited in your usage of your own body parts?
4) How did the group's communication affect its performance?
5) If given the opportunity, what would you have done differently?

"Building a Utopia"

Goal: In this exercise, the groups are confronted with the task of creating what they consider to be a "Utopian" society. The only drawback is that they are forced to create this society as a group, instead of as individuals. This puts their team building and communication to the test.

Direction: (1 hour and 30 minutes)

Split the large group into groups of 6-8. The facilitator should announce to the group that . . .

"Earth is becoming way too crowded. The various world power nations have elected to establish civilization on the moon, finally. The conditions on the moon colonies have been simulated to be exactly like that on Earth. The only difference is the location. The group has been chosen to establish a Utopian society on the moon."

Here is the list of issues the groups have been assigned to sort out for the space colony . . .

How is the government run?
What punishment is there for criminals? If so, what is it?
How are jobs dealt with?
How does one acquire things?
What part does religion play?
What is the role of the family?

How is education dealt with?
What forms of recreation are there?

Small Group Facilitation Questions:

How did you feel about creating a utopia within a group?
How did you feel about sharing your individual utopia?
How do you see our society in relation to your utopia?
What were the most important aspects of your utopia to you?
How did it feel when you didn't agree?
How much of your utopia is framed by your culture, religion or gender?
How did you feel about arguing your point?

A spokesperson from each group should describe their Utopia to the large group. Anyone can question or comment on a Utopia once the spokesperson is finished describing it to the group.

Large Group Facilitation Questions:

How did you feel about this exercise?
How did you feel about the ingredients that made up your utopia, within the group?
How easy/hard was it to come to a consensus about a Utopia?"

"Changing the Game"

Goal: To promote team building through collective thinking and task implementation.

Materials: One traditional and nontraditional sports item.

Directions:

Split the large group into smaller ones. The objective for this activity is for each team to create a sport utilizing both their nontraditional and traditional sports items. They are encouraged to use each item in a creative/unconventional way. They must decide amongst each other how they will use the items and what principals were behind using them in that manner.

For example, if a group at one point decides to toss a bar soap to each member, they might say they chose that action because "it represents the unity that must exist in life for success." It doesn't matter how farfetched the principles are.

After the group has finished constructing their sport, they will have to meet with an opposing team to challenge them with their sport. Each team will have to physically learn the other teams' game. They will share what principals were used and compare and contrast the games that they have created.

After this, all the groups shall come together and perform their new sport in front of the entire group. Once this is completed, the groups will once again separate and begin their small group discussions.

Small Group Facilitation Questions:

How did it feel trying to complete the task?
What role do you think you played in your group?

Large Group Facilitation Questions:

How did your actions help/hinder the group?
If the exercise was repeated, what would you have done differently?

"Dream World"

Goal: To allow the participants to work together in creating and performing a skit.

Directions: (1 Hour and 30 minutes)

Split the large group into smaller ones. Every member in the group must come up with ideas on what they want their dream to be like. Their dream must incorporate a little piece of every person. Together you will come up with a dream that you will later play out in a skit. You will have 20 minutes to come up with this dream. It can be as real or fictional as you decide. There are NO limitations. Then you will be given 15 minutes to find objects that can be used as props in your dream world. They can be objects from the environment, from your rooms/personal belongings. You will have 20 minutes to practice your skit. Try and be creative!

Every group will have 5-7 minutes to perform their skit in front of the entire group.

Large Group Facilitation Questions:

What were some of the things you liked about the other skits?
What issues arose while planning your group skit? How come?
Was it easy/difficult to communicate your ideas with others in the group? How come?
Did the skit come out as planned? How come?
If there was anything you could change about the skit, what would it be? How come?

"Egg Drop"

Goal: This is a two part activity designed to promote interaction, cooperation and trust, through building a structure, then moving into competition.

Materials: Large brown grocery bag, ball of twine, dull scissors, roll of masking tape, newspaper, rubber bands, raw eggs (3 per group)

Directions: (1 Hour and 30 minutes)

To begin this exercise, break the larger group into smaller ones. No larger than 8 per group. Their task will be to create a catcher using the materials given. The groups should be directed to use 10 minutes to solely plan their strategy. After the planning has been done, the next 20-30 minutes are for building the catcher.

There are two things that the groups need to be made aware of.

The catcher cannot exceed the size of the large grocery bag.
The eggs are not part of the design.

The second half of the activity puts the catchers to use. The group will be asked to pick someone who will drop the raw egg from a height of fifteen feet as the rest of the group directs that person.

The different groups will compete against one another to see if they can catch all their eggs without having them break on the floor. After each successful round of egg dropping, the height gets moved higher or until there are no eggs remaining whole.

The purpose is to promote trusting interaction within the bounds of a game. This activity is designed to test how differences in culture/customs affect gamesmanship.

Large Group Facilitation Questions:

What did you like about the exercises?
What feelings come up when participating in an activity such as this?
How did you feel about the competition?
What do you think the purpose of this activity was?

"Group Introduction"

Goal: This group activity is intended to allow different participants to work in a group to achieve the common goal of creating an introduction for the group.

Directions: (1 hour and 15 minutes)

Split the large group into smaller ones. The facilitator will inform the groups that they are charged with the task of inventing an introduction for themselves. This can be done anyway the group chooses. Through dance, song, cheer, silence, with a story, etc. Up to five minutes will be given for each introduction.

Once these instructions have been given, the groups will be separated to prepare for their presentations. 30 minutes will be given for the teams to prepare. The facilitator will periodically check everyone/s progress while informing the groups of the time left.

After the 30 minutes is up, show time begins!

Large Group Facilitation Questions:

What was it like to introduce yourselves as a group?
In what group did everyone fully participate in coming up with ideas?
Who felt pressure to conform to whatever the group decided?

Did people feel like their individuality was able to come out in the introduction?

Who took on the leadership role(s) within the group? How did it feel?

Who sat back and let other members of the group make the decisions? How did that feel?

"Marshmallow Tower w/ Roles"

Goal: To allow the participants to practice working in a group with a common goal.

Materials:

one envelope w/ role cards
one box of spaghetti
one bag of large marshmallows
one bag of mini marshmallows
newspapers to lay on the surface of your building space
large garbage bag (for easy cleanup)

Directions: (1 Hour and 30 minutes)

Split the participants into smaller groups. Take the envelope and have each participant pick a card with a role printed on it. These roles can range from *"team cheerleader, team mole, silent type, loud mouth, team therapist, or teammate hater."* The choice of roles is up to the facilitators. Just try not to have too many destructive roles in one group. This can easily lead the group members to an old fashioned fight to the death which isn't the best activity for "team building".

Make sure to tell the participants to **not** show their cards to other players, even if they ask nicely. Once everyone has been given a role, place a box of spaghetti and two bags of marshmallows in the center of your area. Each group will be given two bags of marshmallows (one large, one medium). They are to utilize their resources to the best of their abilities.

Rules:

Everyone must stay in their role during the activity
No one at anytime should tell what their role is
The object of the game is for each group to build the tallest and sturdiest tower.

This activity works best if participants aren't aware that they are picking out "roles" that will influence their participation in the exercise. Try to keep this a secret for as long as possible

Small Group Facilitation Questions:

Go around in your group and let everyone reveal their roles.
How did you define your role?
If you were to choose your role, which role would it be?
How was the role you were given different from the role you would normally take on?
What role did you see as being a negative role? Positive role?

Large Group Facilitation Questions:

What did everyone think about the game?
How did each group address the different roles?
Let volunteers in the large group reveal what their role was and what role they would prefer.
Discuss some common/different experiences within the groups when building the tower.

"Our Time Together"

Goal: to facilitate teambuilding through trusting, listening and directing.

Materials: Multiple cardboard circles—approximately 16-24 inches in diameter and height. Multiple cardboard cut outs of numbers 1 through 12 with adhesive on the back of it and blindfolds.

Directions: (1 hour and 30 minutes)

Each person will be given two minutes to listen to the directions of their teammates, while they are blindfolded, in order to properly place the number on the clock. Each person on the team will have a chance to put a number on the clock.

1st Round: The first person will start and will be blindfolded. The team will have to guide you as to where the number belongs. If the number is not placed on the clock prior to the 2 minutes, the next person must go.

2nd Round: One teammate must turn the person around the number of times in accordance to the number they are placing on the clock. For example, if you pick number 6, you will be spun 6 times.

Once everyone has completed the clock, the group will sit down and discuss the exercise.

Small Group Facilitation Questions:

How did it feel to be blindfolded while being given directions?
How clear or confusing were the directions?
What has this activity taught you about how you communicate in general?

Large Group Facilitation Questions:

What did you learn, if anything from this exercise?
If there was one thing you could change about this exercise, what would it be?

"Skits"

Goal: To allow group members to create a product in which everyone is involved in creating

Directions: (1 hour and 15 minutes)

Skit A: Split the entire group into smaller ones no larger than 8 per group. Each group is to perform a five minute skit about whatever they choose. The groups have 15 minutes, 20 minutes if extra time is needed, to create a skit.

The skits can be given a theme such as teamwork, leadership, generosity, road rage or fatty foods in America. It doesn't matter. The facilitators can give separate groups various topics for them to cover as well.

Skit B: Give each group a bag of objects that were selected at random. It is important to remember that the items have a specific function or meaning. Have the participants use these objects in the skit in a creative way. It is not mandatory that all objects are used within the performance or everyone has a speaking role. However, everyone should be involved in some aspect.

The main goal of this activity is to get the teams working together and creating a more relaxed atmosphere. The participants must turn out some sort of product, and everyone must be involved in some form.

Small Group Facilitation Questions:

How do you feel about how the group performed?
How did you feel with your personal role in the group?
What other groups do you find yourself involved in and how do they affect you?
What sort of relationships do you have within these groups?
What type of invisible boundaries do you sense within these groups?
What happens when someone crosses these boundaries?
What are your personal boundaries?
What happens when someone crosses your boundaries?

Large Group Facilitation Questions:

How did you feel about this skit?
What has to happen for you to be satisfied with a group?
What did you learn from this exercise?
How did you learn from this exercise?
What else would you like to add?

"Stranded With Strangers"

Goal: This activity will examine how the participants would handle being stranded on a deserted island with their group members.

Directions: (1 hour and 15 minutes)

Split the entire group into several smaller groups. The facilitator will announce that each group has been shipwrecked and stranded on a desolate island. The groups have the choice between creating a new society on the island, attempting to escape, waiting to be rescued or both. Each member must explain what they can possibly bring to the group in efforts of achieving the group's overall objective and well being.

Small Group Facilitation Questions:

How do you feel about being stranded with a group of people that you are not familiar with?
In terms of your own personality characteristics, what can you contribute to the group?
What characteristics would you want that you do not currently have that would help you to get along with the rest of the group?
With the people in this group, how would you determine who would assume what role?
In what other situations have you played this role? What have you learned from that experience?
How would you apply it to future situations?

Large Group Facilitation Questions:

What did you learn about yourself from this experience?
How do you feel about what you contributed?

"Survival Scramble"

Goal: To expose participants to tough decision making regarding the lives of others.

Directions: (1 hour 15 minutes)

Split the entire group into smaller groups. The facilitator will announce that a nuclear missile has been launched and it will be hitting your city in under an hour. The devastation will be catastrophic and impact is imminent. There is a bomb shelter available that will protect you from the force of the missile, as well as the radiation that will be produced from it. The only catch is that there isn't enough room for your entire group inside the shelter.

If your group consists of five people, the shelter should only be able to hold three people. If there are seven in your group, then there should be room for only four people and so on. Depending on the number of people who make it into the shelter compared to those who don't, the dynamic of the conversation and atmosphere of the group will definitely change.

To make things run smoother, appoint a time keeper in each group who will remind everyone that they are on a time limit and a decision has to be made or everyone will perish! If a decision isn't made in the appointed time, no one will survive.

Small Group Facilitation Questions:

How were decisions made?
Who influenced the decisions? How?
How could better decisions have been made?
Did people listen to each other? If not why not?

Large Group Facilitation Questions:

What roles did group members adopt?
How was conflict managed?
What kinds of behavior helped or hindered the group?
How did people feel about the decisions?
What have you learned about the functioning of this group?
What situations at work/home/school do you think are like this exercise?

"Whatever Floats Your Boat"

Goal: To work on communication and teamwork within a group, with a common goal in mind.

Directions: (1 hour and 45 minutes)

The facilitator will tell the group that they are all now part of a social experiment where they must live on an island for six months. On this island we will be provided with all the necessary means of survival (food, water, shelter, clothes).

However, we have decided to build a boat in an effort to return to "civilization". Using the materials provided, we must build a boat that will get the group off the island. (Later, we will test the boat and see if it floats.)

Materials: Twine, balloons, straws, cardboard, popsicle sticks, markers, tape, glue, scissors, rubber bands, paperclips and luck (if skill isn't present).

Next, the group is to decide what five items they wish to have on the island. Not five per person but five for the whole group. Since all the survival items are provided, the group should pick items for moral support, luxury or something beneficial to the entire group. However, no electronics (television, computer, I-pod, DVD player, cell phone, airplane, motor boat, teleportation devices etc) can be brought.

The groups will have an **hour** to build their boat and discuss what items they wish to bring. Once this is done, the rest of the time should be spent in discussion.

Small Group Facilitation Questions: (15 minutes)

What were some obstacles you faced when building the boat?
How did you feel when the group chose to not bring an item you
    suggested?
How did you feel about having to decide on items as a group?
What role did you take when making decisions?
How does that role compare to the usual role you take in daily life?

Once the fifteen minutes are up, the large group discussion should begin. Each group will stand and tell the group about the five items they have chosen to bring and why. Once this has been done, they will place their boats into a tub of water and see if it floats.

"You cannot plough a field by turning it over in your mind."—Author Unknown

RELAXATION ACTIVITIES

"Have the courage to say no. Have the courage to face the truth. Do the right thing because it is right. These are the magic keys to living your life with integrity."—W. Clement Stone

Relaxation activities are designed to help the participants release a lot of the mental and emotional tension that can build up during the program's events. You don't want the participants to head back into the real world confused, emotionally drained and irritable! That's just irresponsible. Ending a program after a closing activity is akin to a plane crash landing without the pilots trying to use its landing gear. The facilitator is the pilot and the relaxation activities are your wheels. Use them when delivering your participants back into the real world.

Relaxation activities should never be the sole form of recreation for the participants. There should be a sufficient number downtime activities planned into the program. Most of the real mental and emotional growth will take place during reflection periods. This process is akin to the science behind building muscles. Muscles aren't built while a person is in the gym sweating, grunting and lifting weights. They are built during rest periods when the muscles are healing from the workout. The same goes for the heart and mind. A lot can be accomplished while we think we're doing nothing.

"Bed Time Story"

Goal: To allow the participants to relax after an intense activity is held.

Directions: (1 hour)

Split the large group in smaller sections. Each person will pick a card from the container, one side has a word and the other side has a phrase. The person will pick either the word or the phrase and begin a story with one sentence with this word **OR** phrase. When they have said their sentence, they will pass the container to the person next to them. The following participants will do the same, starting their sentence after the previous participant's sentence.

The facilitator will ask a volunteer to remember the story in order to repeat it to the large group. (Recording the story with anything other than memory is considered cheating.)

"Embarrassing Revelations"

Goal: To allow participants to share embarrassing stories in an effort to facilitate a more relaxed and jovial atmosphere.

Directions: The facilitator should instruct the participants to sit in a large circle and ask if anyone has any embarrassing stories they'd like to share with the group. This activity can be either hit or miss, depending on the group's level of comfort with each other or their ability to remember such things.

One good way to facilitate the success of this activity is to ask the participants to think about an "embarrassing story" they'd feel comfortable sharing with the group, a few days prior to the actual meeting. This will give people an opportunity to potentially come up with something of substance. Or the facilitator can start things off by revealing an embarrassing "first date" situation (for example) or whatever they have in mind. However, this doesn't guarantee the success of the activity but it will increase the chances.

"Musical Chairs"

Goal: To promote a fun and relaxing atmosphere through light competition.

Materials: Music and chairs.

Directions: (45 minutes)

We all should be familiar with how "Musical chairs" is played but for those who are not, here is how it goes:

Chairs are setup in the middle of the room. They can be in any shape the facilitator chooses. Square, circles, ovals or even a parallelogram are acceptable if desired. The participants should be lined up around the chairs. There should always be 1 chair less, than there are people. So if there are 10 participants, there should be 9 chairs.

Once the music begins playing, the participants are to walk around the chairs. Once the music stops, everyone is to try to find a seat to sit in. The person that is left standing is eliminated. For the next round, one more chair should be removed. If this game is played with a large group, the facilitators may remove multiple chairs in order to move the game along. The rounds shall go on like this until there is only one person left sitting.

Large Group Facilitation Questions:

How did it feel competing for limited spaces?
How did you feel seeing others competing against you? How did this affect you?

For the winner, did you strive to win? How did you achieve this? Was your mind set on winning or just enjoying the experience? How come?

"Speedy Squirrel"

Goal: To allow the participants to relax after an intense activity is held.

Directions: (1 hour and 30 minutes)

Everyone playing the game is sitting in a circle. There is one dealer. He deals each person four cards. Throughout the entire game, each person is only holding four cards. If, for example, there are five people playing the game, there are four acorns in the middle of the circle. The acorns are spread out so that each person is as much within reach of an acorn as everyone else.

The point of the game is to get four of a kind; 5's, four kings, four 9's, etc. The game begins with everyone having four cards including the dealer. However, the rest of the deck remains in front of the dealer. The game begins with the dealer picking up the top card of the deck. He looks at the card and sees if that card will help him get four of a kind.

Let's say, for example, the dealer is holding one Jack, one 10, and two 3's. If the first card that he picks up is a 4 he will pass it to the player to his right. (Cards are always passed to the right). He is not holding any 4's so taking that card will not help him. He then picks up the next card and it is a Jack. He already has one Jack so he will pick up the Jack. But the rule is that you can only hold four cards at all times so he needs to take one of the cards that he is already holding (that he does not need in order to get four of a kind) and pass it to the player on the right.

The player to the right is doing the same thing as the dealer. The only difference is that he is picking up the cards the dealer is passing to him, as opposed to the deck that the dealer is taking cards from. All the remaining players are doing this as well. They are looking at the cards the player to their left is passing to them and deciding if they need that card or not.

Each player is keeping their hand to themselves. They do not want anyone to know if they are getting close to getting four of a kind. If at any point, one of the players gets a four of a kind, he takes one of the acorns from the center of the circle. He does this as discreetly as possible because once an acorn is taken the other players are then allowed to take the remaining ones. But remember there is one less acorn than there are players. Whichever player is not fast enough and does not grab an acorn is out.

Sometimes the players do not realize that an acorn is missing, but the game continues on until all the acorns are taken. The cards are then shuffled and a new round begins. This is done as many times as necessary until there is one winner.

"Twilight Zone"

Goal: To allow the participants to relax after an intense activity is held.

Directions: (45 minutes to an hour)

(This is a guided relaxation exercise). The "tour guide" or facilitator will direct the larger group in this activity while soothing music plays in the background.

> Start off with deep breathing . . .
> Imagine you are someplace . . .
> Where are you?

What do you hear?
What do you see?
What does it smell like?
Who are you with?
What surrounds you?
What are you doing?
How are you feeling?
What made you come here?
What does this place mean to you?
Have you ever been here before?
Now that it is almost time to leave, will you come back?
Once you are ready, open your eyes.
Allow enough time between questions to allow visualizations of the participants to become settled.

Questions for Larger Group:

The questions can be any of the questions asked to the larger group during the exercise.

"Words From the Wise"

Goal: To allow the participants to relax and share quotes with the group.

Materials: Prepared quotes and flashlights

Directions: (45 minutes)

If possible, turn off lights or make room as dim as possible in order to create a serene atmosphere. The person reading the quote will have the flashlight lit on their face. Everyone will form a circle and take turns reading their quote.

After everyone has gone, if time permits, relaxing music should be played as the participants mingle amongst each other and just relax.

"If you wait to do everything until you're sure it's right, you'll probably never do much of anything"- Win Borden

CLOSING ACTIVITIES

What once was will never be again. You can't go back, but just maybe you can make it better.—Sochima Onyekelu-Eze

It would be harsh and irresponsible to send the participants back into the world without a proper "re-entry" exercise.

Compare the facilitators and participants to astronauts who are reentering Earth's atmosphere. Without the proper means of transportation, they'd all burn up, thus making this entire book pointless! However, the *closing activities* function as their Space Shuttle. It will allow for a safe return to the real world. It may not always be a smooth ride, but everyone will make it home.

During the *closing exercises*, the emotions, thoughts and events that emerged during the *opening, self exploration* and *team building* activities are now reflected on. Also, throughout these exercises, participants often confront issues or events from their past that have hindered their lives in some sort of way. The *closing activities* can provoke deep self analysis and if the participant is willing, it can be the first step towards making the change they wish to see within themselves. The skeletons are removed from their closets and placed underground, where bones belong.

An elaborate activity isn't required to end a program. Basic questions concerning the participant's reflections can work just as well such as

"What did you expect when the program began?" or "How does that compare to what you think/feel now?" etc

"Discovery"

Goal: The goal of this activity is to allow the facilitators and participants to end the program by provoking thoughtful reflections.

Materials: Writing utensils and paper

Directions: (45 minutes)

Each person will be given a sheet of paper and writing utensil. The facilitator will ask everyone to write down one thing they've discovered during this experience. It can be one thing about themselves or someone else or the group as a whole. Once everyone has written down an answer, the facilitator will go around the room asking everyone to share.

Large Group Facilitation Questions:

What aspects of the program helped you come up with your answer? How come?
How did your expectations of the program compare to the actual experience?
What does the word "discovery" mean to you?

"Graveyard"

Goal: The purpose of this activity is to think about and discuss situations in our past or present that we want to "bury" or put behind us.

Directions: (1 hour and 30 minutes)

This activity can be done in a large group or the group can be split into smaller ones with no more than 8-10 people. (The smaller one may provide more intimacy and an environment that may be conducive to authentic communication.

Every group will get a shoebox, which represents a coffin, pieces of paper and writing utensils. Each participant should write down the situation they want to bury. Once everyone has done so, the sharing can begin.

Each group member will announce what their situation is and why they're burying it. Once they are done, the will place the piece of paper with the situation written on it, in the shoe box coffin. Once everyone has shared, the box will officially be sealed and never opened again.

Small Group Facilitation Questions:

What is it that you want to bury? How come?
What makes this situation important to you?
How have you dealt with it/are you dealing with it/can you deal with it?
How do you think this "burying" will influence your future?
What have you buried in the past?
How did you bury it?

Large Group Facilitation Questions:

How did you feel about burying your situation?
How did you feel sharing what you buried?
What common themes were there in your group?

"Hard Letting Go"

Goal: This activity assists participants in letting go of negative memories and/or experiences that they wish to get rid of.

Material: Paper, writing utensils, fire and a fireplace.

Directions: (1 hour and 15 minutes)

(This activity is most effective if done at the end of a program, once participants have begun to feel more comfortable with their fellow group members)

If there is a fireplace, fire pit, or any place that allows for fire to burn safely, utilize it for this exercise. HOWEVER, if there isn't such a place where fire can burn safely, PLEASE select another version of this activity or another one in general. Burning down buildings in the name of "self exploration" just doesn't go over to well with the insurance companies.

Keep the entire group together for this exercise. Each participant should be given two pieces of paper. Have each person write down a negative quality about themselves that they wish to change or completely discard, on one paper. On the other piece of paper, they should write a quality they wish they possessed.

One by one, each person will approach the fire pit and announce to the group with vigor and conviction that "I am letting go of _____!! I am replacing it with _____!!" They should explain why in 2-3 sentences then toss the negative trait into the fire.

There are many ways to perform and facilitate "The Hard Letting Go" if fire isn't readily available or safety is an issue. The paper with the negative qualities inscribed on it can be disposed of in various ways. Just be sure that it is an emphatic way of disposal as this action drives the message home.

Large Group Facilitation Questions:

How did it feel to be so open and honest in front of everyone?
What have you learned about yourself or your peers through this exercise?
What else would you like to share?

"Into Reality"

Goal: To allow participants think about things in their lives they wish to make a reality.

Directions: (45 minutes)

The facilitator will inform the participants to think of a goal they want to accomplish. It can be anything from graduating, traveling, getting a better job, losing weight, confessing their love to someone or even writing a book about leadership exercises. The key is for the participant to think of something that they wish and *will* make a reality.

Everyone will be given a piece of paper with the sentence. "I can make ____ a reality."

Everyone will go around the room filling the blank statement. The facilitator should challenge the participants to go out into the world and fulfill these proclamations.

"Life Saver"

Goal: To allow participants to reflect on a possible bond that was created throughout the program.

Materials: Two chairs placed in the middle of the room

Directions: (45 minutes)

The facilitator will ask the participants to think of a person in the larger group who has helped them "survive" the program's experience. Once this is done, the facilitator will select a participant to start things off.

The participant selected will go and sit down in one of the chairs and identify who has helped them survive. That person will then come up as well. The participant will then talk about how this person affected them and what behavior they would want to work on in order to emulate that positive characteristic in that person.

"Medal of Honor"

Goals: The goal of this activity is to allow the facilitators and participants to end the program by reflecting on recent positive accomplishments

Materials: Medals

Directions: (1 hour)

Each participant will come to the center or front of the room and receive a medal. At this time they will wear their medal and award themselves for one positive thing they've done within the last few months to a year. It should be something that is significant to them. They should then explain why it is important to them.

"Our Avatars"

Goal: To allow participants to reveal/confront the real person behind the avatars they hide behind during their everyday lives.

Materials: Balloons and markers

Directions: (1 Hour and 15 minutes)

Instruct the participants that the balloons in front of them will represent the face they wear in public. Once this is said, instruct them to inflate the balloons and draw the face that best depicts who they are on the inside.

Everyone will then present their balloon/avatars, explain it and reveal who the true person behind the mask is.

Large Group Facilitation Questions:

How do you feel about the person behind the mask? How come?
How is this person behind the mask different from the mask?
Are you ready to separate with the mask? How come?

"Don't ask what the world needs. Ask what makes you come alive, and go do it. Because what the world needs is people who have come alive."—Howard Thurman

CONCLUSION

"Don't cry because it's over. Smile because it happened."
—*Dr. Seuss*

We hope the activities you selected from this manual worked for your organization and your group. It is important at the conclusion of any activity; whether it be a one day workshop, or a longer conference or event to provide the participants with a written anonymous evaluation. In order to insure return of the form make sure they are collected prior to the closing of the event. When things are fresh in people's minds they have a tendency to share their honest reactions at the moment. However, if you feel you also want to provide an evaluation later in time when the participants have had the opportunity to reflect and review their experience, then do that also. This might be best one or two weeks after the event. You can then compare these with the evaluations completed at the end of the workshops and/or conference. We have found these evaluations helpful in planning future weekends, conferences and workshops. You will be surprised that issues as simple as accommodations, transportation and food can make a tremendous difference in the reaction of the participants to the program.

We feel that the most rewarding part of the experience for the participants was learning about themselves and others. Most of the participants come back saying that they realized that they aren't so different from the others in the group. Despite the fact that they come from different cultures, races, sexual orientations, religions, socio-economic status and age groups they feel less alone. Many felt that they were unique in their issues, problems and family dynamics and job experiences. After going through the exercises and getting to know others both in the large group and in their individual small groups they come away with a sense of comfort and understanding about themselves and others. To us, this is the joy of providing these experiences.

Be open, be flexible, be creative and don't be afraid to ask for advice and assistance. You will be surprised at the wealth of experience and information that is available when you take a risk and get others involved. When people feel they are invested in the experience they will do all in their power to make sure that it is a success.